DIMMET

Rob Miles is from Devon, and he lives in West Yorkshire. He has taught translation and visual-cultural studies at Leeds, Portsmouth, Hull, and Liverpool universities. His poetry has appeared widely in magazines and anthologies. Rob has won various awards including the Philip Larkin Prize, judged by Don Paterson, the Resurgence International Ecopoetry Prize, judged by Imtiaz Dharker and Jo Shapcott, and the Poets & Players Prize, judged by Sinéad Morrissey.

PRAISE for *Dimmet*

Rob Miles throws light into many mirrors to illuminate the twilit world of *Dimmet*. With great delicacy, he picks out the gleaming detail, from the iris of an owl, 'uploading data/to the moon' to 'the shimmer of her coat, that golden/retro sheen'. Throughout this collection, there is a sense of watchfulness, watching out, being watched. The poems also 'listen as if listening like a mouse/for what is inaudible to most, but is/in fact, that tireless siren song/of the unsprung spring/ of a trap'. In the turn of a line the innocuous image can slide into threat: 'We got on like a house on fire, a home/ablaze'. Through it all, the moon appears and reappears, ancient, new, the eternal Watcher, who keeps coming back to check if we are coming, or if we are still here. This is a beautiful book.
— Imtiaz Dharker

The word 'dimmet' means twilight, and these beautifully spare and spacious lyrics have a glimmering, half-seen quality. The poems make us want to draw close and listen carefully. Alongside, there is wit a-plenty and a deep-felt humanity which can't help noticing and relishing the ordinary and sometimes comical business of being human. I loved Miles's metaphors which are marvellously fresh and bold without being stagey; a bonfire is 'a throng of wood', and a spider a 'brittle stylus' of itself. I will never be able to think of puffins other than as 'whole shelves of Clarice Cliff/flying from cliffs…'. These are poems of great precision and delicacy - with exactly the correct amount of panache!
— Katharine Towers

As a poet, Rob Miles is something of a magician. His poems often begin with apparently everyday situations - a door burning on a bonfire, a neighbour calling down a stairwell - and move through short spaces, but lead us always to somewhere astonishing. How on earth did we get here? a reader of *Dimmet* might ask, and the answer is by the poet's boundless imagination and absolute precision with language. His love for nature, in poems of crows, owls and spiders, is enough to reinvigorate our love for the world. Thank goodness for this voice. Always charming, always musical, these are, like all great poems, things that only this mind could create, beautiful windows we can look through at views - hey, look at that! - brimming with wonder and delight.
— Jonathan Edwards

Dimmet inhabits the edgelands and half-light between lives, but there's nothing indifferent or detached about this finely crafted collection - these are real poems built to function in a real world. Their sheer power insists that we all bear witness, that no one can pretend to be an innocent bystander. When it's done as well as this, there's nowhere on earth poetry can't go.
— John Glenday

A poet of great depth and compassion who understands the paradox in our need to connect with others and the innate solitariness of the human condition. In *Dimmet*, there is a sense of doors opening and closing as meaning shifts and falters, and a translator's intense engagement with language combined with a strong visual sense, which give the poems a marvellously unexpected, cinematic quality: the moon is a 'floating speck on the retina/of the world'; puffins become 'whole shelves of Clarice Cliff'; a spider is 'the bones of a tent/ with its top whipped off.' Fire sparks, fades, flickers and burns through the poems, often flaring into epiphanies, giving the reader a sense of constant anticipation and surprise. Every page is like turning a corner and witnessing a miracle.

— Jenny Lewis

Rob Miles juggles the juxtaposition of an inter-state in many of these poems, balancing cleverly between one situation and another, all with a deft and subtle touch, his trademark wry, dry tone as he wonders about, and explores, a wide range of subjects. And although we see it, we may not immediately understand it, as there are layers to these deceptively simple poems with their clear language and open style. We need to work at interpretation, we can't take what we're being shown at face value. The smooth, calm tone of the poem often belies a great turmoil or devastation below the surface.

— Di Slaney

The prodigious talent of Rob Miles is full in view throughout his remarkable new collection, which ranges widely, ringing the changes on themes of love and loss, place, time, and memory. Whether he is writing about humans, animals, or the land, this very contemporary poet writes freshly, testing the boundaries between self and other. Angry, tender, playful, and at all times empathetic, his poems surprise with their twists and turns of mood and perspective. His command of language and free verse is sure-footed: he keeps line, stanza and metre alive with shifting emotion. Robert Frost urged his readers to 'Listen for the sentence sounds. If you find some of those not bookish, caught fresh from the mouths of people, some of them striking, all of them definite and recognizable…you know you have found a writer.' Rob Miles bears out the truth of Frost's observation, in authentic poetry which is both subtle and accessible. The best collection of contemporary poetry I have read in a long while.

— Lucy Newlyn

CONTENTS

Dimmet

Rob Miles

Broken Sleep Books

ISBN: 978-1-916938-56-4

Cover designed by Aaron Kent

Edited and Typeset by Aaron Kent

Broken Sleep Books Ltd
PO BOX 102
Llandysul
SA44 9BG

For Pip, my family and friends
and in memory of so many.

O white moon, you are lonely,
It is the same with me,
But we have the world to roam over,
Only the lonely are free.
— Sara Teasdale

DELIVERY

Weighing in
at what feels like a month without sleep

his eyes strain
at fresh hex signs on drains

and pavements
and wrapped to a lamppost

a smudged statement
about the crossing. But this morning

all that makes it over
to one of the singing trees

are the finials of a squirrel. Its skipping
pips on a cardio screen

as the postman bends one last time
for his hi-vis bag

plump on the ground like a guide dog
full of where to go

A COUPLE IN THE DARK (NOT REALLY WATCHING *TRISTAN'S ASCENSION* AND *FIRE WOMAN* BY BILL VIOLA)

We can still tell they kiss, soft and slow, cool
as proving dough in this

artificial night, staring not ahead, like us
but finding touch

by touch, how to dematerialise. They don't see
a shrouded man lying down

almost drown, but then ascend as if to rank
among the chosen. Up next

they miss the hooded silhouette of a woman
on a solitary pilgrimage, her arms out wide

she strides and then, with no reflection rising...
dives into an unexpected pool of dark

they might have made out only by the light
of what she left behind in flames.

FAREWELL

Unhinged
                    a door reclines
on a throng of wood: a bonfire
unlit in a garden.

Some reaching twigs completely
without speed, but certainly
by their youthful shape begin

some roundabout escape.
Older branches lightly rustle.
Forklift palettes waffle.

The door is matt
but its blue paint rhymes
farewell to the sky, and it thinks

never mind
            when I burn
                    I will be a sea

WHAT ARE YOU, CROW

if not forever silhouette, even
when the light's
not right? The light

could stare at you
from any side, but claw
and wing

adjusting would still be the confusion
of sharpening knives or fire irons
when you lift...

                           are you the black from flames
                  and the flame
        black flame?

BY CANDLE

To think, you'd tried one on yourself. An intricate
and soundless pair, now unworn

for ever by my bed. Your foot guessed
my temple slipper size, your gift

from the other side of the world
where it seemed we'd been when we took

to a slow dance to test them; your shadow
wild enough to carry on without you

as we all have to.

RUINS

...then weighing up the relics, our luck
and such cliché
as the random lightning bolt

or that runaway bus tomorrow
we stepped out

onto flawless baize
where hearts
and kings once lay, where

all that was left of the abbey
dealt cards of light around itself.

ORACLES

A little over a minute from the first hello
and she hears the phone
being passed around like the eye
among the dreaded.

Greeted by voices
sending love, but picking up
the background chatter, she learns
how one poor soul

had his ear fenestrated
on the NHS, had a tiny window
in his head, though his views
haven't improved

since he'd be *blowed*
if he ever got an appointment again.
He's adamant we'd have been overrun
if we'd voted remain

and then, of course, the teacup chorus:
yes, they say that don't they...
that's right, they do
that's what they say...

ZONES OF EXCLUSION

Where do we reckon
the deadening
starts?

Is it below
the navel, or somewhere
above

the heart?
What test could serve
beyond the neural

byways, the pins
in maps
of connection

or inaction, gathering
where paths
have numbed

at which points
whole parts of us become
closed down to others?

ÓSCAR ALBERTO AND VALERIA

Drowned at the border: father
and daughter, face
down, her arm still
around his shoulder. The image
shared around the world—
not headlines
but punchlines to jokes
about the differences
between the doggy
and the crawl
the backstroke
and the butterfly
and some furious exchanges
about effective parenting styles.

AT SUCH HEIGHTS

                    you could be headlong beyond
any gauge of pain. The pressure up, the oxygen off

your heart starts mumbling molten gold. Your view
now dark but star-shot when the chamber's frame

gives way to memories of rising prayer and nothing
like this simulated climb they've made you take

as you hallucinate those blackened scraps you saw
from dying fires now moths that dust your form as if

for proof to those who watch perplexed and coldly
note your peaceful gaze, that close as they might fly

              to you they've barely changed the air.

WHAT ARE YOU, OWL

if not the wind's wild tuner, unherdable
sky cat? Philosopher
my foot, more the quill-swivelling

killer, all plume-roots and iris. They say
your eyes are too big and round to allow

for much mind, but we all know
you're uploading data
to the moon, winging over frost-

groomed trees and tiles. Folk's fly-by-
night cockerel, yes, we find what's coughed

up, we've seen your dirty tramp-troll
earplug-pellets, we know
you've visited from what you've gifted, itchily

relinquished, your tightly
and politely compacted

capsules of grief, the unholy
remains of bony souls you snared
to swallow, to regurgitate as tufted soundlessness

your dinner made dumb and not listening, listening
like us, not breathing, blue-lipped and hushed

since you don't come near nearly
enough, it has to be you, you, you
                              or air

MOON

Some bad amateur maths pins it at blinking distance.
A hackneyed backlight design for antlers.
Salty ghost sucking crustily on the veins of a tree.

Chimneys giving it the finger get met by nothing
so tough in its serenity. There's no face on this
pick-pocketed fossil, but a face

swallowing a face because no final face
has ever been achieved. It will take much more
than a few kitchen windows to explain. Stare

hard enough through a kettle's breath and the aura
off its rocky iridescence is sticky tape going rogue:
ambiguous attachments, clear

commitment issues, now you see it, now...
Found on baby blue, welcome back as that nightmare
button thought lost in a cot. Singular mother

of all mothers of pearl. Floating speck on the retina
of the world. Eclipses fixed with a quick once over
at the opticians. Slingshot

chalk. Ancient castle moat igniter. Tide-teaser. Sliced
extrusion of seaside rock, blank at both ends
but all the way through saying *moon*.

TSUKUYOMI

He'll descend
shredding the dark. This hunt for himself
in webs

and lakes, in wild unblinking
cats, in skylight cataracts, a night train mistaken
for his stolen necklaces, chasing
reflections in its glass...

                              another brief whirl
                      and slalom across
             the cooling gardens, not one shivering leaf
untouched, no shadow
         unshelled, he'll begin
              a fresh inventory of silks
              and blues
                      his trailing jewels...

but there's nothing, only window mist to greet him.

                                  So, scurrying

as if behind an X-ray safety screen, fingers
to lips
we'll spy
as he slows up, adopts
a gentler step, distracted

takes a nimble

tip

toe

tour

over blank white walls, delighted as a child

observing a hall

of doors

or rows

of little drawers

knowing he'll open all of them.

TEBORI

No petal of moon
              glides this

ink pool. A sky

    blinking itself
          out of itself

          twice

          over the land

    when two bloodless clouds

swallowing stars
          uncurl
             to surface

              like ice-pale koi
at the shadow of his hand

CAMP

Most likely Bulldog, undoubtedly something
brutal

and British, though with no real struggle
or stress for me, except

in my effort
not to get from the middle of that makeshift pitch

to its edge, but for a second
to look up...

                breathlessly. Everyone else

roaring by, but I
stood icon-still, knowing I'd been chosen

for one of my first important scenes— so small
among the big kids, oblivious

to heft and speed, but banking
on the kind of grace and fortitude

fuelling those slow clouds in that blue, blue sky

CATAREEN

She's keeping it down next door.
I never have to strain to hear. Far from it.
Normally everything about her

is too much. If she left, I must admit I'd miss
the boyfriend. The best thing about her
is him

trying to holler her name, Catherine
the French way, *Catarrrreen...* like a moped
hurtling off a cliff, catareening

off a stone face. He can't do it.
But the way he whimpers her name
after tonight's fight, doesn't tickle at all

like what I'd have picked up in this cup
I slid and held on the wall, pretending to the kids
I was taking out a spider.

THE WOMAN FROM ACROSS THE HALL

sends a *hiya!* like a rising then spiralling paper plane
down to where I'm bending, emptying
my cold hot water bottle
into the plant pots
on our communal stairs. She swishes by, followed
by the loyal and delicate ghost
of a woody-oriental scent, *already*
late, mega sexy date, winking
as she descends...

but it's the shimmer of her coat, that golden
retro sheen of the curtains
hanging in my room as a kid, where I'd be
draping myself, or by their silencing light
on brighter days than this
pushing aside set texts
and offers of hanging out
for more *Condé Nast Traveler* tips
or the Great Good Buys
at the back of a stolen *Vogue*.

PENULTIMATES

The night bus ignites a tipsy kissing couple
waiting at the stop after time. Acetylene

in their crystal box, they don't part
until the very last chance she has

to step on, while he
twenty at most, watches with owl eyes

besotted. Melding with the glare of the bus
she's gone, but as it rises

and it dips with the lane, he's left
a spark, lit for a second with his phone.

A SKINFUL

Note the shapes hope assumes
in the knowledge of coming rupture. A clown

brought in to cheer, waves
and turns two hoop-wands, as if to tantalise

and sharpen the fingers of those screaming children
with frogspawn. Let's you and I stroll over

and just lie there too. We may never absorb
the thought of fine grey lightning, backlit

on a dull skull. But now, at least, there's this
lustrous rainbow crazing on something

also taking a skinful, for a moment
holding its own.

CAFÉ POEM

Just when I think there is nothing
so boring

as someone else's childhood
a toddler

in dungarees is guided
around our table

by his puppeteer parent, arms
up, in a vertical sky-dive, or

like a drunk, when walking
is more about not falling

every step forward
rewarded with a double high five.

CHILDREN AFTER SCHOOL

chase and weave
between high hedges, bright

little uniforms bursting
from inside green

and for one second
it's that famous footage

strangely often set
to some guitar classic

or ambient theme
of the napalm bombing

of Vietnam, parents shouting
they must keep up or

Jacob won't make
drama club, Charlotte

will miss choir.
Hold hands.

SUNLIGHT

no longer hesitant in the widening gaps
no longer lost

where spider mites made their thin kingdom
till the tower of it

settled for brown. Little skulls
for flowers by the end. The birds it wore

haven't so much flown
as melted, liquid

quickly. Every sawn
and pointing limb coming plucked

like a feather, replaced
by this fingerless breeze. Staring through

we grow younger, we grew
with this sentinel. These careful, steady cuts

carve the old tree back
to light, more light and nothingness

VIGANELLA

Once upon a shadow
a lofty lobotomy was mooted by one local mayor
to shift the darkness like a mood
to see the sun. He declared his plan

to trepan the mountain
chisel into its tip
to take off its top
so let there be light...

But another
had wisely considered
that a great quilt of mirrors
which tilts upon command

(and not a removal of the block
nor some such brutal extraction
but an optimistic re-use
of the re-thought rock)

would channel the winter sun
like a crackling vintage tune
retouching village faces
with old love or good news.

THE TIME BEING

after Antony Gormley's Maquette for The Brick Man *(1986)*

Guardian or guide between mind
and matter. A thought
unlaunched. Wingless

angel, Christ or Vitruvian man
with his hands
by his sides, indeed

with his hands in his pockets.
Casting no shadow
he'd have marked the moments

for a city. A prototype
though no progeny
outgrows him. How small

we'd make ourselves to enter
at his heel, steps echoing
when we climb

where birds circle
about his ears. Upright
sarcophagus, no treasure but light

left for his afterlife
where he will always stand
for an idea.

WHAT WERE YOU, SPIDER

if not the unflushed hauled back up
on luck and your knee-knuckles? Not much more
than the bones of a tent
with its top whipped off. Breeze-

dried through, you retuned
as the many-armed harpist, all prongs for strings
to pluck to shivers, to strum
in sun for a day. At first you lived giddily

on a windowsill, then on tenterhooks
on a thinning crochet clinging to its pin, catching
airborne banquets, falling
horizontally. Rain came

lending globes for your orrery, but the cold
made your domain craze
like a trodden mosaic, overcrowded now
with no guests and no busy maker

except what's left in the neatening frost
in which you've formed, like grief, this brittle stylus
of yourself, this crisp claw
to needle an infinite spiral.

GNOMON

Confound him too
Who in this place set up a sundial
To cut and hack my days so wretchedly
Into small portions!
— Plautus

i

The fanciest cake slice left
slicing into icing— eternally weight
not clock watching.

ii

Sail gone up in a lake of brass. Birds
at least twice the boat's size
figuring how to land.

iii

By day, an oblong gong, small reward
for a job well done; by night
RMS Titanic going down.

iv

In the Forbidden City, eternity pinned
its spinning top; clocks elsewhere
are wick, water, incense, sand.

v

In his circle, a sorcerer summoning
from beyond, grimoire and wand shaking
to make tell the light.

vi

A fin tells endless beginnings, forever
in motion; moonlight
keeps even a shark's ghost going...

vii

Bright as the metals bent for war
on Vulcan's anvil in Velázquez's forge—
all moments froze when Apollo spoke.

viii

A brutalist tube not looked into
but claiming it can tell perfectly well
where it stands. Dumb telescope.

vix

Like Urizen's tool, but unhinged
measuring days not space; darkness
will be half this compass.

x

Ornate and inviting
as the wrought-iron gate to a garden
tended by forgetfulness.

xi

Snow over the numbers, grubby bear
gauging depth not hours, this being
the countdown.

xii

Red-hot spike on the dial. Untouchable
ragged shadows— forest fire
tearing time to now.

DIMMET

His hands still bronzed, still
baling-raw. His voice
no longer snared, whisper-low
as decades ago, in this same field, he guided me

to not disturb that horse; circling
quietly, its half-scattered straw
an ingot melting, and my thin flames no match
for such a sunset anyway.

*

On this, another near-to-night, it's clear
that he has no more kept his mind
from wayward sparks than I
have closed my eyes

before any fading fire, ever since recalled
a slow white shadow
steady on its dial
in the always almost dark.

UNDERTAKINGS

We pray you'll flicker here, long beyond
the city-bitten rest of us.

For us
you're the one who's found a way

despite unspeakable loss. You've survived
outside time, still binding

priceless tomes for palaces, still baling
bales for old and unclaimed horses

waiting in their breath each day
for you, for your kindness, for your sunrise hair.

CAPTIVITY

Cut from her stride, she is knuckle-rooted
fist-steadied on all-fours. The belly of her
slung M flexes upward, inward

and holds. Her arms have the girth of old
jetty pilings, fur like woken iron filings.
Unmoved juggernaut. She sniffs the dead

eye of the lens, twitches her wide black
heart within black heart, its hard-
won symmetries stirred then firm again

like drying tar. She burns air with a stare.
With a blink she lets go her grip
on our turning world. Everything is caught.

UNDER THE THUMBS

Just above the water: my ten toes. A distinct arch
in a hot heaven of foam. Both little toes
particularly little, noticeably curled. The next
equally unusually permanently bent
and so on. In summer sandals, once
a friend pointed out how I must have spent my childhood
in badly fitting shoes. I didn't
correct him. But even in a distant city
and decades away, I wouldn't admit to lying
about the pressure of the thumbs
whenever mum pushed down firmly
all around the edges as if
to seal a pie. To get my choice, as she judged
the various pairs I'd picked to try
had plenty of room to grow in, I'd have to trudge
for months, toes splayed or scrunched
to hold them on, to save, to prove she wasn't wrong.

FOR US, BROTHER

it was all fists and sun, who could take it
or have to break away. Hands down
as kids it was torture

tournaments on hot car bonnets, or tarry
prints on everything from digging up
the brand-new path

for loaded games with giant farmyard steel
wheel bearings, or my vision
cobwebbed in an instant

on that garden chipping freed and
ricocheting from your new Black Widow
catapult, then my steady nails

in thoughtful retribution, pushing
through the taut tissue on the body
of your balsa wood planes, or our small palms

crossed with heated coppers
as we scrapped for scalding pennies
scattered at the fair around the old

town crier's boots, or scoring broken Bic
tattoos with still-stinging quills
around shadow, knuckle

and spasm, or flint-sharp sticks swiping
at the lucky tracer sparks
whirling in a storm of dirty light

behind a tractor on its tilting
lap of honour, fuming past us holding up
its torch of cooling hay.

SMALL DEVICES

He packed, but forgot
what one, maybe
both, later stopped

with a blow, brushed
into dust, left for decades
on that shelf

as their young hearts
slowly swapped
for either tired little motors

cooling off, or
small devices
ticking, only time would tell

HIS NIBS

Though no saint, he has his cross to bear, and this
handles like a relic, but then that

isn't really the word.

                                 I'm page testing
                   this shiny corporate pen he's sent

with his company's name
in a dignified, curling script along its polished barrel.

                       And I'm pondering pride

and irony, given the condition of the kind
I know for a fact

he will usually use, still managing
                 that business at home— every last nib
                      pressed and pushed
                         a little bit out of true.

KNOW THYSELF

Who could've imagined her there? Barely
a footstep beyond
her road, next thing, haggling like a pro
on that white island—

too hot, roasting most of the time, grandma
pretended to moan
while watching me unwrap
the ceramic reproduction

of a charioteer, handing me another round
of my first ever taste
of pitta and taramasalata, then sliding me
the card

depicting that famously engorged
priapic satyr, watching
for my reaction, guessing
it better to deliver in person than post.

I WHISPERED TO THE DOG

that she'd been a winner
a Crufts champion

at least twice. Once
she saw off a Dobermann, burglars, a werewolf

even the odd Sasquatch.
I reminded her

as her old eyes darkened
that she had saved lives.

FROM Z TO A

In Spanish, it goes *tho-O*: every letter is said. So
it's *tho*, as in *think,* with an unvoiced *th*, without

the *ink*, and then the *O,* as in the *O* of *O please
can we go?* It might be practised along with *zorro*

by beginners. *Zorro* means *fox* and is pronounced
exactly like *tho-O,* apart from the voiced, rolling

trill in the middle à la Eartha Kitt, who loved men
and this brings us once again to Antonio Banderas.

HONOURING THE ANCIENT DEAD

No matter what you see of age
or illness, disaster, ritual, or war, remember

while you learn, no fragments found
behind this glass

could be my love, nor all my knowledge
nor all yours.

You may not chance to share
this air, although you might reflect

the heart and vision that you are
is also how I was. Release for me at least

a breath, a tiny, living wish for peace. Then breathe
as if for all of us.

CONJUGATIONS

We must, of course, thank the French for nailing the terms for times
like these: the universal in-betweens. *Par example,* the *petite mort.*

The most vivid works have always caught a touch
of it (or rather, we should say of *them* and their metaphors).

Art's two eternal subjects (and their cognate adjectives, nouns
and verbs) gasp, curl and conjugate in us when one

the other, or even both occur (as above). So often tangled in lines
of fire, or earth, or air, or water (then in flames

and worms, and birds, and waves, and more) are love
and death, said any way but straight, kinking on the tongue or page

of anyone who's yearning for (or cannot but express) that *je ne sais...*
that certain breathlessness.

PARTS OF US

...and thinking myself alone
I turned to see thee still awake, likewise
staring starward. Caution
overboard, we started to make up
new nonsense words
or reworked all those terms
to claim, like bits
of ships, those parts of us
that bear no name. My thanks indeed
for such *scudgels*, then I gifted thee
thy twisted *bunths* between
our bodies *frondling* in their *remainbrace*. I kissed
thy *forebow* better, that is
thy tidal frown, our teeth forsooth
a kind of offshore skirmish made...

(and there must be a word
for that unnerving smirk
new couples share when drowning)

A GATHERING

Taking the long way from the stones, your boot
barely spared the skull of a bird
on dense pine needles. We paused

to take it in, the two of us alone composed
a gathering, enough
to seem a crowd looking down

on that fallen cradle.
Save a few last stains, its raw hollows
had been picked dry, pestered

almost clean, and it still hosted a ghost of gnats
making all known holy signs
over what remained of body

and wing. You kneeled so gently
to bring its tiny silence home
where any sound found every nook

and corner; every pindrop rose
as each room lowered into
night's wide water.

TRIVIA

I really snarled at you.
You've squirrelled yourself away.

I tidy about you now
sleeping

paws peeping just over the duvet
your head buried

from my trivia. And you've left
your shoes, which I asked you to move, to sort

once and for all, one on top
of the other

as if to take up
even less space.

SO YOU'VE RISEN

robed
but unmoving

at the end of our bed
in the small hours. Again

                                    you'll wait for me to see

the light, demanding
silently

what went right in our world today.

                              One more tiny hell.

For once I'll lie
and tell you I slept.

                        So much begins

and ends like this.

                        Always

some immaterial thing

                              made flesh in wordlessness

MAKING WAY

A keeper, you said of the house, but I'd sensed everything
trying to make its way: those errant velvet fingers
from your orchid pots; the oak
putting on its chain mail of ivy and moss
and losing; the birds we fed still pinned
to their shadows; crisp wasps
electrocuted by views
through grubby double glazing, and you
just weeks before, showing your wrists
as if uncuffed, asking for my thoughts on a fragrance.

HOUSE AND HOME

We got on like a house on fire, a home
ablaze. We lay down
in our ruin, let that tasty air
nourish old flames amongst other
rubbish. It sucked up enough
of next door for an even bigger
claim, body-bagged us two firemen
a valiant passer-by, and one old woman
rushing in to save the cat (another little bag
for that). We scorched us
a pit in the earth as deep
and crumbly as a grave, knew ashes
for kisses when nothing
remained, a pyre dying
on a hill, a black hole on the estate
like any good home thought safe
as houses, brought down, eaten
out of, where the heart is, furiously
played, we lit it with love, we lit it with hate.

THE STOPPER

lifted, and all we did
undoes, unfixes

beneath this weight of days retuned
to weightlessness

in wilderness, each field
or beach

and every forest found, that late night bath

we ran, my fingers parting
tangled strands, our tracks

in crops or sand

then every moon phase

slowly foaming over
your sore shoulders, risen blades

of floating grass, the hidden notes
all unforgotten, unshared
thoughts

and thoughts

where I drift, but stand

suspended

WHAT ARE YOU, PUFFIN

if not our prodigal punk?
Underground and smuggling nothing
then for years you'll wing it

piercing and weaving through wave
under wave as much as above.
Late last spring, your folks

were Mayfair billionaires, burrowing:
no pool or gym, but one cracking
Fabergé permitted and out pops

a puffling looking knackered already
in a knee-length fur.
You've no plectrum-shaped face

nor proper orange swimming fins yet.
Though up and down you'll plod
meaning serious business

in someone else's flip-flops.
Yes, you're getting the eye:
each worried iris in its tiny triangle

that symbol of providence
on the back of a one-dollar bill
like the secret of your own bill's

counterfeit shades exposed
one psychoactive day under ultra-violet
bright as a barbecue brick.

In daylight at a distance
great circuses of you
become flung crockery

whole shelves of Clarice Cliff
flying from cliffs, wild fragments
crashing back to land, legs wide

as a clown off a slide
for more kinky beak butting
clocking up the molecules with a kiss.

(There are myths too, of a culinary kind:
your hearts dished up raw, so it's told.
And while you should grow old

in old puffins' homes, you can't grow tall
or cast vast fishing lines
and so you wash ashore in scores

wasting away with the ice
down to its own last bones.)

IKTSUARPOK

If, toward the precipice of an age
as strange as this

this
might seem a loss, discernibly
failing faculties or

a giddiness
before some party
you're hoping you'd throw

and not
your truly wolf-like hearing, acute
to the point of supernatural

but merely you
who finds you
wandering outside

past those weary fairy lights, every once
in a while, then know you

have not stood alone, blinking
into cold and endless
emptiness

but have joined us
keeping watch for each seed of star
any mote of moon.

TO LISTEN FOR A MOUSE

means to get mouse-like, and a mouse
must know its own sound better
than the many bigger beings, better
than any system set
for its detection. A mouse
must calculate the weight
and tension of its very soul, the tickling
resonance of its ribcage, any
tendency or potential
for scratchiness; it must match claw
and grip and speed to the depths
and textures of all surfaces.

To listen for a mouse
means to map from memory
where you stood still last, or crept
to where something scuttled, to that place
another, not too dissimilar
and possibly even quieter
did not come back, not even
as a ghost, but had itself failed
to listen as if listening like a mouse
for what is inaudible to most, but is
in fact, that tireless siren song
of the unsprung spring
of a trap.

IN ONE INSTANCE

it is said

outer space has a scent

of spent gunpowder— imagine

the spitting barrel, a bullet

sent, but in this case

the bang

and the echo

and its echo

and an ozone aroma are the heralds

not the trace

then so many puny hairs teased

to leave their roots

ushered

willingly, a wish

ungranted, that fat genie suddenly

siphoned back

to his lamp, this snipped-off

bungee of screaming light, ragged feather, reaching

leafless

branch, though the soul

of a plumb-line, always

to the same curse rising

when spilling wax

over careless hands— to liquify by fire or pestle

its prey when it does

and does not quite kiss down

tentative

and opposed as either one

            of those backwards-

       forwards toes

of the chameleon's grip, or the tip

                 of a whip, or a gymnast's ribbon

          when it reaches

             but reacts

                 retracts

                     to be exact

         to make certain, making certain, making

contact

THIS CRYSTALLINE FIELD

                          had given up

on flowers

but rests now, recovers
in the glow of its own surprise

at a high summer day without rain.   So far

so cliché...

                but that's nothing
to what the moon will make of this.

ACKNOWLEDGEMENTS

My sincere thanks to the editors and judges at the following publications and organisations who kindly gave time and space to some of the poems in this collection:

Ambit; *Angle*; *The Anthology of Light* (Black Light Engine Room); *The Anthology of Love* (The Emma Press); *Borderlines*; Carers UK; *14 Magazine*; The Gregory O'Donoghue International Poetry Prize; The Guernsey International Poetry Competition; Honouring the Ancient Dead; *The Interpreter's House*; *Live Canon Winners Anthology 2012*; *Lunar Poetry*; *Masculinity: An Anthology of Modern Voices* (Broken Sleep Books); *Mediterranean Poetry*; *Militant Thistles*; *Morphrog* (The Frogmore Press); *New Boots and Pantisocracies*; *New Welsh Review*; *Obsessed with Pipework*; *One Hand Clapping*; *Orbis*; The Philip Larkin Society; *Poetry News* (The Poetry Society); *Poetry Wales*; Poets & Players; *Remembering Oluwale: An Anthology*; The Resurgence Prize and *Resurgence & Ecologist Magazine*; Segora International Poetry Competition; Seren Books; *The Scores*; *Somewhere to Keep the Rain: Winning Poems from the Winchester Poetry Prize*; *Spelt*; *Stand*; *Ten Poems about Brothers* and *Twenty-One Poems about Wonky Animals* (Candlestick Press); The Walter Swan Poetry Prize; *Welsh Poetry Competition: An Anthology of the Best Writing from the International Welsh Poetry Competition (2017-2021)*.

My thanks especially also to members of the Otley Poetry Stanza, led by Jane Kite, and Cut Loose organised by Dean Parkin and Michael Laskey, and to all at Broken Sleep Books.

LAY OUT YOUR UNREST

www.ingramcontent.com/pod-product-compliance
Lightning Source LLC
Chambersburg PA
CBHW020216090426
42734CB00008B/1102